Decoding Fairytales
Chris Knight

Part I
The Sleeping Beauty and Other Tales

The Sleeping Beauty tells of a king and queen who yearned for a child. Eventually, a baby daughter was born:

> *Her parents celebrated with a feast, to which the Wise Women were invited. There were thirteen of these in the kingdom, but since the King had just twelve golden plates, one would have to be refused.*
>
> *The feast was held in splendour, and the Wise Women bestowed their blessings on the child. The youngest ensured that she would grow up to be the most beautiful woman in the world, the next promised that she would have the spirit of an angel, the third gave her grace, the fourth decreed that she would dance perfectly, the fifth that she should sing like a nightingale. And so the blessings went on. But after the eleventh fairy had bestowed her gift, the doors of the banqueting hall suddenly flew open and the thirteenth fairy burst in. Seeing that no place had been laid for her, she turned her blessing into a curse. 'The King's daughter', she declared, shall in her fifteenth year prick herself with a spindle and fall down dead.'*
>
> *Having uttered her terrible curse, the thirteenth fairy disappeared. The king and queen were distraught, and everyone was crying. But the twelfth Wise Woman, whose blessing had yet to be given, came forward to offer help. She had not enough power to undo the evil spell, but she could soften it. Instead of dying when she pricked her finger, the girl would now only sleep for a hundred years.*

The good fairy cast her benign spell, but the King was still not satisfied. He determined to evade the consequences of the curse: every spindle in the whole kingdom was to be burnt; on no account was his daughter to bleed.

When the girl came of age, however, the inevitable duly occurred. On her fifteenth birthday, when the King and Queen were not at home, Beauty was exploring the great palace. She came to an old tower. She climbed up the spiral stairway and at the top reached a little door. Pushing this open, she found herself in a little room; and there inside was an old woman with a spindle, busily spinning her flax. Fascinated by the spindle merrily rattling round, the young girl reached out to grasp it – and pricked her finger. She began to bleed, and fell into a deep sleep.

The curious thing was, however, that the dreadful event did not simply send the girl herself into the world of dreams. It affected the entire palace and the entire kingdom. All normal life was suddenly terminated. The King and Queen, who had just come home, fell into a deep sleep along with the whole of the court. The horses slept in the stable, the dogs in the yard, the flies on the wall – all stopped where they were. Even the fire that was flaming in the hearth went still, and the cook, who was just going to hit the scullery boy, let him be and went to sleep. Everyone joined the princess in her magical trance. It was as if time itself stood still.

For a hundred years, all were frozen in their positions. And as the years passed, an immense forest surrounded by an impenetrable hedge of thorns grew around the palace. In the surrounding neighbourhood, people almost forgot about the existence of the mysterious palace deep in the woods.

Yet legend maintained that behind the hedge of thorns was a palace in which lay a sleeping princess. From time to time, young men on hearing the legend would attempt to cut their way through the hedge in order to win the reputedly-lovely sleeping bride. But each would-be suitor was caught in the thorns, which clutched together as if they were alive. As the years passed, more and more suitors were trapped and died.

At long last, when a hundred years had passed, a suitor who had heard the legend decided to try his luck. This time, as he approached the hedge, large and beautiful flowers replaced the thorns, and the branches parted of their own accord to let him through, closing again as he passed. He found the palace, entered inside, stepped over sleeping bodies and eventually found Beauty herself. He kissed her, she awoke from her sleep, the entire palace woke up with her, the two were married and the couple lived happily ever after.[1]

Blood, time and 'the curse'

This narrative is entirely and consistently menstrual. Like Jack-and-the-Beanstalk, Little Red Riding Hood, Cinderella and countless others of its kind, it is about 'this world' – the world of ordinary marital and domestic life – about 'the other world', and about the transition between the two. 'The other world' is a strange place of enchantment in which marital sex is impossible. It's the kingdom of death. All fairy tales involve a journey between life and death. Something triggers this movement, and the most potent trigger is a flow of blood.

Let's look again at *The Sleeping Beauty*. In approaching the symbolism, we may begin with a passage by Bruno Bettelheim:

> 'The thirteen fairies in the Brothers Grimm story are reminiscent of the thirteen lunar months into which the year was once, in ancient times, divided... the number of twelve good fairies plus a thirteenth evil one indicates symbolically that the fatal 'curse' refers to menstruation.'[2]

The background is the perennial problem of how to fit a fixed number of lunar months into the 365¼-day solar year. 'The earliest calendar year', writes Emily Lyle, 'was not the solar year of 365 days, but the lunar year consisting of twelve lunar cycles, to which an intercalary month was generally added every two or three years to keep the months in line with the natural seasons'.[3] The number of days in a lunar cycle varies between twenty-nine and thirty – on average 29½ – so that a year was either 354 days (twelve lunar months) or 383½ days (thirteen lunar months). In other words, for as long as the year was divided up into observational lunar months – a sequence of directly-observed 'moons' – there was no way in which the number '13' could be avoided. At the end of each twelve moons, a part of the thirteenth always made its presence felt, and some place for it in the calendar had to be found. The only way to establish the solar year as fixedly consisting of twelve month-like periods was to divide it into schematic 'months', arbitrarily adjusting the length of each to ensure that twelve of them totalled just 365 days. This, of course, is a feature of the modern Christian (Gregorian) calendar. The thirteenth month has been effectively suppressed. In folklore, however – at least in Europe – the suppressed month, and with it the number thirteen, remains associated with those older pagan traditions which took account not only of the sun but of the moon as well. This liminal, half-excluded thirteenth month finds reflection in 'the persistence of the number thirteen' as the standard number of 'witches' ('Wise Women' or 'Fairies' as Grimm's tale puts it) in a coven in pre-Christian European traditions of ritualism.[4]

A dispute also exists as to whether menstruation should be considered a blessing or a curse. Retaining consistency with our previous analyses,[5] we will assume the existence of an early tradition according to which menstrual bleeding was associated with the moon – and therefore with the number thirteen – and was considered a manifestation of women's ritual power. Menstruation was, in other words, included among all the other blessings a young woman could have. Since it promised fertility, it may even have been the ultimate blessing. The newer custom – and certainly the Christian one – has been to attempt to suppress mentrual bleeding just as the thirteenth month has been suppressed. In both respects, lunar time is being denied.

This, then, is the background to the story. The story itself tells of how a king and queen attempted to reject the blessing of menstrual bleeding altogether. All they wanted – or rather, all the king wanted (for we are not told of the queen's attitude in all of this) – was for the baby daughter to grow up as a perfect wife. The blessings given by the 'good' fairies are all 'marital' ones: they are the attributes which any would-be suitor would look for in a bride – good looks, grace, dancing skills, a melodious voice etc. etc. No husband would be attracted by the menstrual condition of his bride, so the thirteenth fairy with her own special gift is spurned. The king, we are told, has only twelve places laid.

But the menstrual blessing cannot be ignored. If suppressed, it simply makes its presence felt in malevolent form. It takes on the nature of a curse. Menstruation in its normal or traditional form is a periodic but purely temporary 'death' to marital and domestic life. The injured and angered thirteenth fairy utters her curse: when the girl comes of age, no force on earth will prevent her from bleeding. But in this case, as a punishment, she will bleed until she dies.

The commutation of this death sentence determines for the princess a fate somewhere between normal monthly seclusion and permanent death. Her seclusion will last for a hundred years. And the penalty to be paid by the king and queen is to be subjected to the full rigours of the traditional menstrual spell – in exaggeratedly prolonged form. The traditional logic was for menstruation (particularly, we might suppose, that of a princess) to cast its spell widely over society, the ban on marital sex lasting for several days (or at most a fortnight). Assuming our theoretical model of culture's 'initial situation',[6] the sex-strike launched society each month into a profound process of metamorphosis, as profound as the switch between waking life and sleep. But this certainly didn't last for a hundred years. The century-long seclusion featured in *The Sleeping Beauty* is a community's punishment for its attempt to escape seclusion altogether.

The menstrual spell is a cyclical occurrence, just as is seasonal change. Time, in the traditional view, is itself cyclical. The king, in attempting to destroy all spindles, is attempting to suppress the spinning by women of the threads of time – threads which wind like yarn around a spool. We may also infer that he is hostile to 'spinsterhood'. A traditional occupation for unmarried or secluded women may have been spinning, so that a woman who never married became seen as permanently a 'spinster'. Be that as it may, when the princess explores the unfamiliar stairway and discovers the old witch spinning flax in her turret in the sky, she is contacting the other world and discovering for herself the guardian of her fertility. Like the thirteenth fairy, this old woman brings menstruation as a gift – or, when rejected, as a curse.

The girl 'pricks her finger.' She bleeds, as any girl of her age eventually must. The King was foolish to try to banish the spinning-wheels or spindles. Time cannot be suppressed – every girl will come of age and bleed, her cycle itself being among the most ancient of all clocks. And as the princess bleeds, the ancient power of the blood strikes out with a vengeance against all who had believed they could defy it. The whole palace, the whole kingdom is plunged into another realm beyond waking life. All normal domestic activities cease. It is as if time stood still. Those who believed that they could alter the ancient calendar, they could abolish the thirteenth month, they could suppress the hallowed logic of menstrual time are now put firmly in their place. They will be excluded from time's flow for a hundred years.

As the princess sleeps on, it is as if her blood had erected around her an impenetrable barrier to her ever getting married. Would-be suitors are kept at bay by a deadly hedge of thorns. She herself is now in menstrual seclusion of a particularly rigorous and enduring kind, with the whole palace in seclusion with her.

But every period of seclusion – even a hundred-year one – must eventually expire. And when the time has come, lovers are free once more to embrace. The spell breaks, the thorns turn into flowers. The hedge parts, allowing the young hero to enter and deliver his kiss. The period of seclusion is over; the servants resume their domestic chores. Marriage is celebrated with a royal wedding and feast.

Jack and the Beanstalk

Two versions of this story will be drawn on here. The earliest known published edition appeared in London in 1734, under the title *Enchantment demonstrated in the Story of Jack Spriggins and the Enchanted Bean*.[7] However, this version seems to have been forgotten; all later tellings seem to derive from one printed much later – in 1807. This was a sixpenny booklet called *The History of Jack and the Beanstalk* and is abridged below.[8] It should be added that another version published in the same year – *The History of Mother Twaddle, and the Marvellous Achievements of Her Son Jack* – is very similar but ends with Jack killing the giant and marrying the damsel who had welcomed him and protected him in the giant's house.[9]

The 1734 publication is significant in that it is the earliest known version, and substantially different from the others, allowing a perspective on the familiar versions which all stem from the same printed source.[10] In this alternative version, the motif of incest is stressed. We are told that although Jack 'was a smart large boy', nevertheless 'his Grandmother and he laid together, and between whiles the good old Woman instructed Jack in many Things...' The woman says to her grandson:

> 'Jack, says she, as you are a comfortable Bed Fellow to me, I must tell you that I have a Bean is my House which will make your Fortune....'

The old woman accidentally loses the bean from her purse; it falls into the ashes of the hearth, where the cat finds it just as Jack is making his grandmother's fire:

> 'Odds Budd', says Jack, I'll set it in our Garden, and see what it will come to, for I always loved Beans and Bacon; and then what was wonderful! the Bean was no sooner put into the Ground, but the Sprout of it Jumped out of the Earth, and grew so quick that it gave Jack a Fillip on the Nose, and made him bleed furiously....'

Bleeding 'furiously' from his nose, Jack runs to his grandmother crying 'Save me! I am killed!'; she tells him that now her enchantment will be broken in an hour's time, whereupon she will be transformed. Angry at Jack's theft of her bean, she attempts to thrash him, but he escapes up the Beanstalk, which is now a mile high. As her hour expires, the old woman turns into 'a monstrous Toad' and crawls into a cellar on her way to the Shades.

Meanwhile Jack climbs and climbs. On theoretical grounds, we know that food should not be available to him, on account of his nose-bleed.[11] Little attention is usually given to the motif in the familiar version in which Jack (after a scolding from his mother) is sent 'supperless to bed.' In fact, however, there is more to this than meets the eye. The version we're now examining lays laborious stress on Jack's hunger, which afflicts him from the moment he begins to bleed. Jack calls at an inn in a town on one of the beanstalk's leaves:

> 'Here he thought to rest for a Time, and goes strutting like a Crow in a Gutter: What have you to eat Landlord, says he' Everything in the World, Sir, says the Landlord: Why then, says Jack, give me a Neck of Mutton and Broth: Alas, says the Landlord, to morrow is Market Day, how unfortunate it is' I cannot get you a Neck of Mutton to Night If it was to save my Soul: Well then get me something else, says Jack. Have you any Veal? No, indeed, Sir, not at present; but there is a fine Calf fatting at Mr. Jenkinson's, that will be killed on Saturday next. But have you any Beef in your House, says Jack? Why truly, Sir, says the Landlord, if you had been here on Monday last, I believe, though I say it that should not say it, you never saw so fine a Sir Loin of Beef as we had, and Plum Pudding too, which the Justice who dined here, and their Clerks and Constables entirely demolished, and though I got nothing by them, yet their Company was a Credit to my House! Zounds, says Jack, have you nothing in the House? I am hungry, I am starving....'

Jack hears a cock crowing and demands that this be killed and broiled; the Landlord refuses because the cock 'belongs to the squire'. Jack asks for a hen to be killed; but all the hens are incubating eggs, which should hatch in a week. 'Have you no Eggs in the House?', asks Jack. 'No, Sir, indeed', answers the Landlord, 'but Jest Eggs, which we make of Chalk'. 'Why then', says Jack, 'what the Devil have you got?' 'Why to tell you the Truth, Sir, I don't know that I have any thing in the House to eat...' At this point, the narrator explains: 'Thus was poor Jack plagued by the Enchantment of his Grandmother, who was resolved to lay him under her ill Tongue, so long as her Power lasted.'

At last, however, the old woman's spell breaks; at this point, the marital phase is entered. While the old grandmother turns into a toad, Jack finds himself at last in the presence of the opposite kind of woman – a 'fair lady' known as the 'Empress of the Mountains of the Moon'; in her previous life she was the grandmother's black cat. It is explained that this beautiful woman is entirely at Jack's disposal, and that he now has the full power to enjoy every imaginable pleasure. The couple go to bed and 'play their Rantum scantum Tricks until the next Morning'. Jack is so tired from his amorous exertions that he sleeps long into the morning, dreaming about killing the giant Gogmagog and rescuing 'several thousand young Ladies' from being crushed in the monster's jaws.

* * * * *

The later version will be more familiar. Jack sells his mother's cow 'for a few paltry beans', which the old woman angrily throws into the garden. Having nothing to eat, 'they both went supperless to bed'. In the morning, Jack sees a huge beanstalk growing in the garden and climbs up to the sky. Jack finds himself in a barren world: 'he concluded that he must now die with hunger.' He arrives at a castle and is taken in by a woman at the door; she agrees to hide him in the oven where he will not be seen by her husband, a giant who likes human flesh. The giant enters, declaring he can smell fresh meat, but Jack remains safe in the oven. Having eaten his usual cannibalistic meal, the giant falls asleep. Jack escapes, seizes a magic hen which lays golden eggs and climbs down the beanstalk with his prize to his mother.

Some time later, Jack resolves to climb up again. His mother refuses permission, so Jack 'rose very early, put on his disguise, changed his complexion, and, unperceived by any one, climbed the beanstalk.' The change of complexion is achieved with 'something to discolour his skin.' He is soon back at the castle, unrecognised by the giant's wife. Events are repeated – this time with Jack stealing gold and silver in two bags.

On the third trip to the sky, it is midsummer's day. Jack disguises himself completely, goes to the castle and this time escapes with the giant's magic harp – magic because it plays all by itself. The harp cries out to warn the giant, who wakes up and chases the boy down the beanstalk. But as Jack reaches the ground he fetches an axe, chops down the stalk and brings the giant crashing to his death. Jack and his mother live in wealth and comfort to the end of their days.[12]

Discussion. Bleeding from the nose may be regarded as a technique of 'male menstruation' (nose-bleeding for this purpose is common in Papua

New Guinea).[13] The story of Jack and the Beanstalk may in this light relate to some long-forgotten tradition of male initiation in England.

The relevant menstrual magic is stated in the myth to be derived from womankind: Jack acquires the bean from his grandmother, or in exchange for his Mother's cow. He is under the spell of this incestuous relationship as his nose bleeds and as he climbs the beanstalk. The immense, growing beanstalk doubtless has phallic connotations. These, however, are inseparable from the incest-motif: the magic is sexual, but it is also menstrual and symbolic of the mother-son connection. This is not marital sex.

While blood is flowing, flesh is raw and inedible, so hunger logically prevails. While under the spell, correspondingly, Jack is hungry (this is stressed in all versions) and when he arrives at the castle be is in fact (to use the language of so many Australian Aboriginal myths) 'swallowed'. He is taken into a cooking receptacle in the giant's kitchen. Far from eating meat, he himself *is* the meat. He comes frighteningly close to being eaten alive. His flesh is raw, the odour of blood exciting and arousing the giant. 'Fee! Fi! Fo! Fum!', as the English Yurlunggur[14] thunders in the pantomime versions, 'I smell the blood of an Englishman.'

Three trips are made into the giant's kitchen, and three treasures stolen. When Jack 'changes his complexion' and hides in a symbolic womb (the oven) he is undergoing a role-change similar to that undergone by women in entering menstrual seclusion. When he emerges and escapes from the monster's jaws in possession of the treasures, it is as if he were reborn. The stolen goose, gold and harp take the place of the stolen blood and fire – or the stolen sound-making instruments or ritual paraphernalia – as featured in primitive matriarchy myths the world over.[15] Why three trips to the sky? A lunar/menstrual interpretation would be that this is because once a month, the moon is absent from the sky for a period which corresponds, ideally, to the time of the menstrual flow. The 'third time lucky' motif derives from the idea that the moon is 'lucky' – i.e. it arises from its temporary 'death' – on the third night after its disappearance.

Once Jack has gone up three times, he chops the beanstalk down, ending the menstrual/incestuous spell and the possibility of further journeys to the sky. A lunar interpretation can be placed on the fact that this occurs on midsummer's day. When the lunar light/dark cycle is mapped onto the seasonal cycle, midsummer appears as 'full moon'. This is the traditional time of emergence from seclusion – a moment often marked by ceremonial love-making.[16]

Little Red Riding Hood

If Jack-and-the-Beanstalk relates, possibly, to an ancient English ritual of male initiation, Little Red Riding Hood by the same token probably relates to a female counterpart – a young woman's first menstruation rite.

This tale, which has a long French tradition, was told from the late Middle Ages up to the present. Its prominence between the fifteenth and seventeenth centuries was connected with the great superstitious belief in werewolves current in the period. In the course of numerous trials, men and women were persecuted and killed on the charge of being secret wolves.[17] Werewolves, as is well-known, appear to be human until they undergo a metamorphosis and reveal themselves temporarily to be wolves, the process being connected with the changing phases of the moon.

Menstruation is associated with the idea of temporary death – death followed by rebirth. It may also be viewed as a change of 'masks', 'skins' or roles (the 'change of complexion' in Jack-and-the-Beanstalk is a male version of this). In retreating into seclusion together, women lose their former identities and become incorporated (as if 'swallowed) into a larger identity of both human and animal 'blood'. When they emerge once more, they regain their separate identities as if being regurgitated and restored to new life.[18]

The focus of dramatic interest in Little Red Riding Hood is the extraordinarily-changed appearance of what the heroine takes to be her grandmother. The old woman has suddenly grown enormous eyes, ears and teeth, as well as a ravenous cannibalistic appetite. In the early French oral versions from which Perrault derived his familiar literary tale,[19] the werewolf invites the young girl to join in the cannibalistic feast. The wolf

> ' ... arrives at the grandmother's house, eats her, and puts part of her flesh in a bin and her blood in a bottle. Then the little girl arrives. The werewolf disguised as the grandmother gives her the flesh to eat and the blood to drink.'[20]

The little girl unknowingly eats her grandmother's flesh and drinks her blood.

Like Jack's nosebleed, this detail once again indicates the power of the theoretical model. It expresses the basic structural fact underlying all these tales – namely, that in order to travel to the world beyond (in order to be initiated) what's needed is blood – in this case, maternal blood. The maiden's 'red riding hood' may be regarded as symbolic of this.

Zipes points out that the blood-drinking episode 'acts out an initiation ritual...'[21] 'In facing the werewolf and temporarily abandoning herself to him', he continues,

> 'the little girl sees the animal side of her self. She crosses the border between civilisation and wilderness, goes beyond the dividing line to face death in order to live.'[22]

Seeing 'the animal side of herself' is explicable in the template's terms: to menstruate is to bleed 'as if' bitten by a wolf. It is to adopt an identity symbolised by blood and shared by women and wild animals alike. 'Facing death in order to live' refers us once again to menstruation as a 'temporary death' anticipating rebirth.

In the familiar version, the cannibalism motif is less explicit, but both the girl and her grandmother are conjoined in 'excessive' maternal intimacy (reminiscent of Jack's incest) in the monster's belly. They emerge once more as separate individuals only after the wolf is cut open and they are rescued. From this point on, the girl enters a new life. As Bettelheim comments:

> 'Little Red Cap and her grandmother do not really die, but they are certainly reborn. If there is a central theme to the wide variety of fairy tales, it is that of rebirth to a higher plane.'[23]

* * * * *

Cinderella

The following is Charles Perrault's version of this 'best-known fairy story in the world'[24]

> There was once a girl who lived among the cinders of the hearth place and was called 'Cinderella' as a result. Her mother had died and her father had remarried. Her step-mother and two step-sisters continuously taunted and exploited her: it was they who forced her to wear rags and to sleep in the fireplace.
>
> One day a royal ball was announced. The two step-sisters and the step-mother dressed up in their finery; Cinderella was forbidden to go. While everyone was at the ball, however, Cinderella's fairy godmother appeared and conjured up a magical means of travel to the ball, together with clothes of silver and gold cloth. Unrecognised, Cinderella arrived in splendour at the royal palace and danced with the prince. The spell broke at midnight, whereupon Cinderella had to run home in rags, leaving her glass slipper behind. The prince toured the kingdom, searching for the woman whose foot would fit the slipper he had retrieved. At last, he arrived at Cinderella's home. The step-sisters tried on the slipper in vain, while Cinderella's tiny foot fitted perfectly, qualifying her to become the prince's bride.[25]

The spirits of blood and fire

The dramatic interest of this story centres on the relationship between Cinderella and her step-sisters. A vast number of versions of Cinderella have been recorded.[26] In all of them, the contrast between the 'good' and the 'bad' bride or brides can be shown to concern the contrast between two fundamental roles of womankind, who (from a male standpoint) is either 'attractive' (available as a bride) or 'unattractive' (connected by blood to her own kin).

Cinderella's association with fire is unambiguous. Even if we leave aside versions in which she is explicitly the bringer of cooking-fire to a cold hearth,[27] the evidence is plentiful. In the familiar version, she sleeps every night in the fireplace; in a Scottish version, she hides 'behind the cauldron'[28]; in an Armenian version, she 'sits in the stove'.[29] In short, there is no doubt that she is, as Cox puts it, 'the guardian of the hearth'.[30]

Role-exchanging is also a prominent theme. In some versions, the 'good' and 'bad' sisters exchange dresses, so that one is taken for the other.[31] Even in the familiar version, Cinderella is unrecognised by anyone at the ball. All this makes sense given my model of the initial situation for human symbolic culture. The exchanges of roles, slippers and clothes express a lunar logic of metamorphosis and alternation between opposed states associated with 'fire' versus 'blood' as symbols of *marriage* and *kinship* respectively.

What is certainly noticeable is that Cinderella lacks menstrual attachments or solidarity. She is detached (by death) from her mother and also gets married; the other two sisters (note that there are two – their sisterhood defines them) never marry. They stay with each other and with their mother. That is, they put kinship soldarity first. Recall my model of culture's initial situation. Following through its implications, we expect Cinderella to be 'cooked' as a mark of her marital availability. By the same token, the other two sisters should be 'bloody' and 'raw' – attached in the first instance to their own blood.

The fact that Cinderella's flesh is 'cooked' is suggested unequivocally: Cinderella sleeps every night in the fireplace. But do the other sisters really menstruate?

The answer is that they do. In Grimm's version – paralleled in this respect by hundreds of others[32] – the following events take place during the final slipper-trying episode. The king's son has arrived with the slipper, which the two step-sisters are determined to try on:

> 'The eldest went with the shoe into her room and wanted to try it on, and her mother stood by. But she could not get her big toe into

it, and the shoe was too small for her. Then her mother gave her a knife and said: 'Cut the toe off; when you are Queen you will have no more need to go on foot.' The maiden cut the toe off, forced the foot into the shoe, swallowed the pain, and went out to the King's son'.[33]

The prince now rides off with the eldest sister. However, they have to pass the grave of Cinderella's mother, on which grows a tree with two pigeons perched in its branches. As the prince and his bride pass, the pigeons expose the false bride's bloody secret. They sing out to the prince:

*'Turn and peep, turn and peep,
There's blood within the shoe,
The shoe it is too small for her,
The true bride waits for you.'*

It is therefore not because the sister is 'ugly' that the prince rejects her. In fact, he is perfectly prepared to accept her as the beautiful young maiden with whom he had danced at the ball. He rejects her purely and simply when he is informed that she is bleeding from her 'shoe' (an obvious vagina-symbol[34]). Grimm's narrative continues:

'Then he looked at her foot and saw how the blood was trickling from it. He turned his horse round and took the false bride home again, and said she was not the true one.'

The other sister tried on the shoe and – when it did not fit – cut off her heel. This, too, deceived the prince until he was informed by the pigeons of the blood in this sister's shoe:

'He looked down at her foot and saw how the blood was running out of her shoe, and how it had stained her white stocking quite red. Then he turned his horse and took the false bride home again. This also is not the right one, said he...'

Cinderella is summoned and the shoe fits her like a glove. 'No blood is in the shoe... The true bride rides with you...' the two pigeons confirm.[35]

So Cinderella is 'cooked', whereas her sisters' wounds make them bloody and raw. An Icelandic version clarifies this still more starkly. Two sisters are sent off to fetch cooking-fire from the cave in which it dwells, but each comes back unsuccessfully – one with a cut and bleeding hand, the other with her nose bitten off. The beautiful youngest daughter, however, arrives in the cave, finds the fire, cooks some bread and meat 'well and carefully', and returns home with the gift of domestic fire. She then marries a prince who, in his former incarnation, had been the terrifying monster guarding the fire in his dark cave.[36]

Not only is Cinderella 'cooked', whereas her step-sisters are bloody and raw – she is also shines bright whereas her rivals are left in the dark. Grimm's version describes how Cinderella's dress, when she goes to the ball, is woven out of gold and silver. A Norwegian version specifies that the three dresses correspond to 'sun, moon and star'.[37] The bleeding sisters, by contrast, in Grimm's version have their eyes plucked out by the two pigeons which settle on each of Cinderella's shoulders as she gets married in the church. Just as Cinderella (in Grimm's version) had been forced by her step-mother to separate a bowlful of lentils from the ashes into which they had been thrown, so now the prince has separated lightness from the dark, beauty from ugliness, 'the good' from 'the bad.'

A further feature in Grimm's Cinderella is that the royal ball lasts for three nights. Three times, Cinderella's appearance is transformed; three times, she dances with the prince in her dazzling finery but is recognised by no-one; three times she runs home afterwards to hide, allowing her face to become dirty and putting on rags. Cinderella's three trips between home and the ballroom and her disguising of her identity match Jack's repeated trips up his magic beanstalk and his discolouring of his face to avoid being recognised. In Cinderella, too, the motif of incest is present. The 'ugly' sisters are associated with 'blood' and matrilineal kinship; Cinderella has no female kin and instead prioritises marriage. Not only is she not incestuous: she makes a strong point of escaping from incest – the motif of Cinderella's father's incestuous advances and her escape is quite explicit in numerous versions.[38] In Grimm's version, she has to repeatedly run from her father who turns out to be in league with the prince in attempting to catch her before she is ready. Fortunately, she escapes, in a process which involves not merely hiding but also the exchanging of one identity for another. After the ball, the prince tries to accompany her home:

> 'She escaped from him, however, and sprang into the pigeon house. The King's son waited until her father came, and then he told him that the unknown maiden had leapt into the pigeon-house. The old man thought: 'Can it be Cinderella?' and they had to bring him an axe and a pickaxe that he might hew the pigeon-house to pieces, but no one was inside it'.[39]

Cinderella has escaped through the back, left her dazzling dress on her mother's grave and seated herself back among the ashes in her grey gown. This happens twice. It is only on his third attempt that the prince succeeds in catching Cinderella, by pouring pitch on the staircase of the ballroom so that her shoe gets stuck in it for him to retrieve. The suggestion is that Cinderella is only ready for marriage after her three trips to the ballroom and her three escapes. It is all a matter of timing (as Perrault's version confirms, with its story about Cinderella's obligation to return from the ballroom at midnight). Had she allowed herself to be caught earlier, this would have been to violate the special three-day period of magical self-transformation which she had been given by her mother's spirit. Once her three days of disguises, escapes and hiding are over, marriage can properly ensue.

Part II

Amerindian variations

In each one of our four fairy tales, then, blood casts a powerful spell. It carries away young men or maidens from marital bliss into another realm. That enchanted kingdom is an inversion of the normal one: instead of eating, the heroine is treated as food; instead of marrying, she returns to the womb; instead of being awake, she is immersed in deep sleep. And the process of moving from world to world involves a profound transformation of the self: the heroine falls into a deep trance or sleep (Sleeping Beauty), the nose bleeds, the face is blackened (Jack-and-the-Beanstalk); huge eyes, ears and teeth render the familiar face unrecognisable (Red Riding Hood); dazzling clothes and finery suddenly turn back to rags and vice versa (Cinderella). There is a moving to and fro – or a bobbing up and down – between opposite states:

> Cinderella: between dazzling splendour and dark humiliation or even blindness, between fire and blood, between marital union and the bonds of kinship, between the 'true' bride and the 'false';
>
> Jack-and-the-Beanstalk: between earth and sky, poverty and wealth, mother's hearth and giant's oven;
>
> Red Riding Hood: between the real mother-figure and her false counterpart; between the inside and the outside of the wolf's belly;
>
> Sleeping Beauty: between sleep and waking life, stillness and movement, curse and kiss,

Of course, in any conceivable plot or story-line, events must occur, and it would be easy to compare and contrast these with one another in various ways. This in itself would prove nothing. Any tale whatsoever would be consistent with the theory that contrasts of one kind or another can be discerned.

More interesting is the fact that magical tales conform to a definite pattern of constraints. By 'magical tales' I mean stories of a particular kind — those purporting to explain the origins of ritual power. Magical tales are those originating within the context of magical ritual; they are stories designed, literally, to enchant.

In this context, the narrator is *not* free to invent any sequence at will. My whole argument would be demolished if, for example, a single accurately recorded traditional magical tale depicted a maiden bleeding during her honeymoon. In every case without exception, it will be found that blood triggers not marital sex but its opposite – *incestuous* intimacy, union with an *animal* spouse, conjunction with *death* and so forth. Moreover, whenever a contrast pair – raw versus cooked, for example – enters the story, it matters which way round it appears. Let's assume for the moment that menstruation is coded negatively, as it usually is. Then the choices include:

Menstruation	Emergence from seclusion
Raw	Cooked
Blood	Fire
Wet	Dry
Darkness	Light
Incest	Marriage
Kinship	Affinity
Hunger/being eaten	Feasting
Curse	Kiss
Ugliness	Beauty
Rags	Riches

Suppose the story teller were completely free. Then items from either column could be selected at random and strung together to form a plot. In fact, however, rigorous constraints apply. A hero cannot marry his bride only to discover that he is hungry or being eaten alive.

Hunger goes with menstruation, not marriage. A plot about a supperless wedding might make an interesting story – but as magic it wouldn't work. For enchantment to take effect, the signals on either side must be distinguished from one another and transmitted loud and clear. Marriage, cooking and feasting amplify one another and should therefore go together, just as incest, rawness and hunger go together. This is because menstruation ruptures marital sex, generating kinship solidarity in its place. For people who live by hunting, success in the hunt depends on community wide solidarity. Cooking, feasting and marital enjoyment depend upon a successful outcome of the hunt. If marital sex were permitted prematurely – *before* a successful conclusion of the hunt – then the sequence would be thrown into chaos. This initial situation – it is here argued – is the point of departure for human ritual symbolism generally. If the theory is correct, it should be preserved and replicated in mythology across the world.

The story-teller, if all this is accepted, cannot take one element from either column without suggestive reference to the others. Of its own accord, incest *brings to mind* associated motifs such as blood, hunger, rawness, return to the womb and so forth. Contrariwise, marriage *brings to mind* domestic bliss, cooking, feasting and so forth. This doesn't mean, of course, that each and every item must be explicitly included in each and every telling of the tale. The story-teller has much freedom in this respect: he or she can select which themes to emphasise. For example, a choice might be made as to whether the story concerns the struggle between beauty and ugliness, or the conflict between earth and sky. Is the story about light versus darkness, or fire versus blood? These kinds of choices can be made. But once selected, each bi-polar term has to be correctly arranged. No-one has ever heard of a menstruating cook, a marriage celebrated in the belly of a wolf, a true bride whose bridal gown is stained or a false bride who remains in purest white, menstruation on midsummer's afternoon or a honeymoon during an eclipse. It is often thought that in magical myths, anything at all is allowed. In reality, the constraints – although seemingly subtle and unobtrusive, and although they have previously eluded precise specification – are rigid, consistent and identical throughout the world.

The bird-nester

The subject of *universal* constraints shaping the construction of myths brings us to Claude Lévi-Strauss' monumental study of North and South American Indian myths. The 'key myth' of the four-volume work is a tale told by the Bororo Indians of Central Brazil.[40]

> *In olden times, the women used to go into the forest to gather the palms used in the making of penis-sheaths which were presented to adolescent boys at their initiation ceremony. One youth secretly followed his mother into the forest as she did this, caught her unawares, and raped her.*
>
> *As punishment, his angry father forced him to steal three noise-making instruments (a bell and two rattles) from the souls inhabiting the other world. The boy journeyed three times to the land of the dead, returning safely with the trophies thanks to the help of various animals who took his side.*
>
> *Then his father made the boy climb up a steep rock-face to the sky, using a pole as ladder. The father claimed that some macaws were nesting in the face of the cliff and the boy was to capture them. But when the boy had reached the nests the father knocked the pole down, stranding the bird-nester in the sky.*
>
> *Feeling hungry, the boy set off along the top of the rock and began to look for food. But when he had killed some lizards, which he strung around his waist, they went rotten, producing such a smell that he fainted. While he was asleep, vultures – attracted by the rotting meat – came and ate the lizards, and then began eating the boy himself. His hindquarters were completely gnawed away.*
>
> *Before they had devoured him completely, however, the vultures lifted him into the air and deposited him at the foot of a mountain. The hero regained consciousness 'as if he were awaking from a dream.'*
>
> *Having tried to eat food without success – the food passed straight through his body without being digested, owing to his lack of a rectum – the boy moulded himself an artificial behind of dough. Having thus stopped himself up, he ate his fill.*
>
> *When he returned to his village, neither his grandmother nor his younger brother recognised him – he looked like a lizard. However, he revealed himself to them, resuming his human appearance. That same night, a violent thunderstorm extinguished all the fires in the village except his grandmother's. Next morning, everybody had to come to her for hot embers to rekindle their fires.*

Finally, the hero changed himself into a deer and rushed at his father who was out hunting, killing him. The boy dropped his dead father into a lake, in which cannibalistic fish devoured all but the bones.

The boy then killed his father's wives, including his own mother.

Discussion

The Bororo story of the 'bird-nester' can be interpreted as follows. We may think of it as an American Indian version of Jack-and-the-Beanstalk. In both stories, we have an incestuous relationship with the mother (with the implication that mothers cannot be trusted to control their own sons). This is followed by a trip to the sky, hunger, the experience of being treated as food, descent from the sky and revenge upon the personage held responsible for the suffering endured. In both cases, we have the motif of three trips to the other world, and the stealing of three trophies. And in both cases, we have a disguised reference to male menstruation: in Jack-and-the-Beanstalk, Jack's blackening of his own face (in the familiar version) or his nosebleed (in the earliest published version) connotes 'skin-change'; in the Bororo 'bird nester' story, we have the hero's lack of a behind and consequent incontinence. In his own analysis of this myth, Lévi-Strauss[41] links menstruation (as a potentially-excessive degree of 'openness') to various other kinds of 'incontinence' or 'lack of control over bodily orifices'. Certainly, the condition of the Bororo 'bird-nester', whose food runs straight through him as if he had no rectum at all, would be a familiar initiatory experience in the eyes of many South American tropical forest peoples. The next section below will illustrate this with an example from the north-west Amazonian Barasana, among whom male initiation involves drinking yagê – a beer which induces diarrhoea.[42]

In order to emerge from her seclusion, a menstruating woman must, in effect, cease to be 'open'. She must, so to speak, stop herself up. At the end of his ordeal, the 'bird-nester' stops himself up with a behind made of dough; it is suggested that in this, he is mirroring the role of a menstruating girl stopping up her flow as the condition of emergence from seclusion.

The Bororo bird-nester makes a sequence of moves, each quickly followed by its opposite. He goes to the land of the dead, but comes back miraculously alive. He climbs a steep cliff-face, but is later carried down again. He has his hindquarters removed, but then succeeds in stopping himself up with dough. He is slowly eaten alive, and is unable to eat food himself, but later eats his fill. He faints, then wakes up. Rains fall, putting out almost all the fires, but on the following morning the fires are all kindled again. The hero becomes a lizard but then resumes his human form. These changes of state can be tabulated in this way:

First state	Second state
Death	Life
Sky	Earth
Open	Closed
Eaten	Eating
Hungry	Full
Asleep	Awake
Rain	Fire
Animal form	Human form

The elements in the first column are all those appropriate to death or return to the womb, while those in the second connote emergence or re-birth. The boy brings on his first experience of death by his initial act of incest with his mother. The myth doesn't tell us whether the hero eventually finds a wife, but we know that he negates the possibility of any further return to the womb: he goes to the extreme of killing his own mother. A further reversal concerns his relationship with his father. Initially it is his father who sends him to the likelihood of a watery death (the land of the souls can be reached only by flying over a lake) and who subjects him to the suffering of being eaten alive; at the end, the boy drops his dead father into a lake where he is eaten by carnivorous fish.

Male menstruation among the Barasana

Lévi-Strauss does not interpret this myth in the context of male initiation ritual. Nonetheless, it can be shown that the elements in the first column above correspond to the experience of entering the seclusion of a male initiation rite (or the seclusion of menstruation), while those in the second column correspond to emergence from this state.

The Bororo bird-nester myth is explicit about its own connection with male initiation ritual. As the myth opens, the boy is about to be initiated. Why? The myth immediately provides an answer: the youth rapes his mother as she is obtaining the necessary penis-sheath. Women, then, can't be trusted to (or don't have the strength to) control their adolescent sons. Men must therefore do it for them. So the boy's father takes the necessary action. The young bird-nester's adventures are a punishment for his incest, and, we might say, take the place of his initiation. He would have been initiated; instead he is sent to the world of the dead, stranded in the sky, eaten alive etc. We may take it, then, that these adventures are in fact a coded reference to the experiences involved in initiation itself. The bird-nester's temporary 'death' (encounter with 'rottenness', fainting, being eaten etc.) followed by 'rebirth' (waking up, resuming his human form etc.) would then correspond to the usual logic of male initiation-rites.

In this context, a detailed account of Bororo male initiation ritual might help us in understanding the myth. The anthropologist J. Christopher Crocker gives a sketchy description based on informants' memories: initiation involved an encounter with the *aigé*, a kind of Bororo Rainbow Snake.[43] Lévi-Strauss writes that this monster gave off a vile stench of rottenness; it lived in rivers and marshlands, and its voice was the sound of the bullroarer.[44] Australian and Amazonian analogies would lead us to expect an equivalence between this vile-smelling *aigé* and the 'smell' and 'rottenness' of 'death' associated with menstruation.

Given the difficulties in reconstructing an adequate picture of Bororo male initiation, however, we may at this point turn for help to one of the most thorough modern studies of male initiation ritual to have been conducted in the South American tropical forest region. This is Stephen and Christine Hugh Jones's account of *'He* House' among the Amazonian Barasana. In addition to being good ethnography, this happens also to be one of the few accounts of fieldwork in South America designed to test some of the theoretical findings made by Lévi-Strauss in his *Mythologiques*.

'He House' means 'menstrual house' – or rather, it means the large communal dwelling in which men menstruate in a seasonal ritual designed to bring on the annual rains. The rite of *He* House is in essence a three-day collective menstrual period undergone by men. It is of particular relevance to my thesis, not least because on the level of symbolic intention, everything which happens in northern Australian male initiation ritual is precisely mirrored among the Barasana, although the materials and techniques used in embodying these intentions (for example, the use of red paint instead of blood or ochre) do differ from their Australian counterparts.

Prominent in the rite of *He* House are a variety of flutes and 'trumpets' (in fact large megaphones). These trumpets, which represent a great Snake – an anaconda – produce 'a terrifying noise', compared to thunder; this noise is made by the player blowing with pursed lips down an open tube 'and is thus like an amplified fart'.[45] A feature of the trumpets is that they are 'open-ended'; they are said to 'open up' women at puberty (causing them to menstruate). If a child should see the trumpets (or other *He* instruments), its anus would be disastrously opened up – it would suffer from violent diarrhoea until it wasted away and died. Consistently with this, initiation – which involves contact with the trumpets – does 'open up' boys (rather – we may note – as the 'bird-nester' has his behind eaten away). A feature of *He* House is that the participants drink *yage* beer to give themselves diarrhoea. It also makes them vomit. It is clear that this male activity of self-opening and cleansing by the release of vomit and excrement is conceptualised as a counterpart to the more natural 'self-purifying' process of female menstruation.[46] A girl's vagina is 'opened up' for the first time when she reaches puberty and has her first menstrual period; certain myths say that the first 'opening up' of women for menstruation was achieved by means of the trumpets.[47]

As I pointed out earlier, in four of our most familiar European fairy-tales, blood is involved in casting a powerful spell. This is certainly the case – at least metaphorically – in the rite of *He* House The climax of the rite is the melting of beeswax in a sacred wax gourd. The wax 'has a specific association with menstrual blood', while the gourd container is 'like a womb containing children'. The melting of the wax produces a symbolic menstrual flow which brings on the annual rains.[48] During the ritual, the novices and others are covered with red paint 'identified with menstrual blood';[49] women are not to touch this paint or they 'will immediately start to menstruate', their blood being this paint.[50]

He House is not only a 'metaphorical menstruation',[51] it is also 'a symbolic act in which adult men give birth to the initiates'.[52] In order to give birth, men 'must first be opened up and made to menstruate'.[53] The boys to be born are metaphorically 'swallowed' by an immense snake – an anaconda.[54] The boys are coated with black paint, associated with both menstruation and periodicity.[55] 'Black paint is the colour of rottenness and death, and makes the wearer dead'.[56] The boys are then 'sat down....in a foetal position with their knees drawn up to their chests'.[57] That is, they are now foetuses inside the maternal womb. It is an extremely vulnerable condition – an exposed state which is 'compared to that of crabs and other animals that have shed their old shells or skins'.⁵⁸ This is linked to the belief that menstruation, like *He* House as a whole, 'is an internal changing of skin'.⁵⁹ The boys in their vulnerable condition are like crabs – or like menstruating women – in the process of self-renewal. The boys are subsequently reborn and are then carried by the men exactly as if they were newborn babies. Finally, they are ritually 'cooked' by being bathed in smoke.⁶⁰

In her discussion of the logic involved in all of this, Christine Hugh-Jones notes the contrast between the organised reproductivity of men and the isolated, randomised reproductivity of women. The nub of the matter is that *He* House as 'male menstruation' brings men together as an organised group – in starkest contrast with female menstruation, which 'sets women apart in an order which is purely random from the social point of view.'⁶¹

In order for the rains to be brought on, then, collective menstruation must somehow be organized. It is an implication of the myths that originally, this task was performed by women. In the beginning, say the myths, came *'Romi Kumu*, Woman Shaman, the prototype shaman from whom all shamans derive their power...'⁶² Using her magic vagina, which contained alternately water and fire, she created the seasonal cycle by first submerging the world in a flood, then burning it in a universal conflagration.⁶³ The rainy season is 'the menstrual period of the sky',⁶⁴ the rain itself being *Romi Kumu*'s blood. The time of the onset of the rains is associated with the Pleiades and with the moon;⁶⁵ among the neighbouring Desana, this is the moment when the huge anacondas rise up vertically out of the water to 'assure themselves of the changing seasons'.⁶⁶

The shedding of the blood-like rain is conceptualised as a cosmic renewal, a moment of 'cosmic skin-change', consistent with the idea that *He* House 'succeeds in renewing the natural processes of the world'.⁶⁷ The renewal of women, being associated with the moon, is also associated with the opposition between day and night; it is equally associated with the alternation between wet season and dry.⁶⁸ *Romi Kumu* is old in the evening, yet by painting herself with menstrual blood and then bathing to wash it off she 'changes her skin' and becomes young again each morning.⁶⁹ Seasonal and lunar rebirth or renewal express the same logic in which death is overcome. These notions are summed up by Stephen Hugh-Jones when he writes that women

> 'are semi-immortal: through menstruation, they continually renew their

bodies by an internal changing of skin – hence they live longer than men – and through childbirth they replace themselves with children. These processes are thought of as being akin to the succession of seasons and the growth of animals and plants in the natural world. The key to female creativity is seen to lie in the fact that women, like the world of nature, are periodic and cyclical.'[70]

The myths say that the ancestors of humanity had the chance to remain immortal but lost it by failing to adequately respect *Romi Kumu's* womb. Woman-shaman had offered men her immortality-conferring 'gourd' (that is, her vagina). However, men's response was unwise. 'I'm not going to eat from your vagina, it is very bitter and smells', was the response of Old Star when offered the gift of eternal life. *Romi Kumu* therefore put the magic gourd back between her legs and offered men an imitation.[71] This is the gourd used in the ritual of *He* House today. It is 'not the real one but the left-over gourd which gives life but not immortality'.[72] It is said that when men foolishly declined *Romi Kumu's* offer, snakes and spiders stepped in, ate from the 'smelly' vagina and acquired the gift of periodic skin-changing as an alternative to dying. Men were left only with the artificial gourd. Since then, when men have died, they have not come back to life.[73]

The boys who, in the ritual, are coated with black paint and are said to 'die' and then 'come alive', are said to be following in the footsteps of the Moon, who was the first to die and be reborn in this way.[74] Yet the men know that what they do is in some sense only an 'imitation' of the real thing. 'We were directly told', writes Christine Hugh-Jones, 'that *He wi* is like women's menstruation but that women really do menstruate while *He wi* is *bahi kemoase*, imitation'.[75] The women say: 'The men make as if they too create children but it's like a lie'.[76]

The interchangeability of myths and rites

The Barasana have their own rich corpus of myths through which to conceptualise and organise the experiences involved in *He* House. However, it hardly seems to matter which magical myths are selected as keys providing access to the secrets. I will now argue that since all magical myths derive from the same template, and since this template is also the point of departure for the corresponding rituals, a good fit is guaranteed in advance. In fact, almost any fairy-tale from neighbouring tribes – or even from European folklore – might seem valuable to the

Barasana as a window into the secrets of *He* House. To say – as will now be argued – that the Bororo 'bird-nester' myth might be similarly informative is therefore not to make any special claims about this particular myth. Almost any other fairy tale might work. Still, this one works beautifully, too.

Let's recall the key features of the 'bird-nester' myth: the hero's maternal incest and rape, his punishment by his father, his three errands to the world of the dead and so on. Although some inventiveness and shifts of emphasis may be required, we'll see that it's not difficult to settle *He* House into the conceptual box provided by this myth.

Without claiming complete ethnographic fidelity at every point, here's one way to establish such a fit. Beginning with the incest-motif, we're forced to concede that no Barasana boy would in real life rape his mother in the course of being initiated. But the ritual of *He* House (a) brings a boy into intimate contact with 'menstrual blood' and with a 'womb' from which he is 'reborn' and (b) gives him power over all women, including his mother. In the rite of *He* House, no Barasana boy – to continue – would be punished by his father by being sent on three errands to the world of the dead. But each *He* House novice is compelled to spend three days in a menstrual hut in which he symbolically joins the ranks of the dead. He comes back from this seclusion in possession of the emblems and paraphernalia of male ritual power (rather as the 'bird-nester' returns with two rattles and a bell). No Barasana youth has to climb a cliff-face to the sky. But entering *He* House is certainly travelling to another world. The 'bird-nester' is deceived by his father, who knocks away the pole and thereby imprisons his son. Deception of the uninitiated is an important element in *He* House as in all male initiation ritual; and once in the secluded sphere, no escape is allowed before the allotted time. The 'bird-nester' is extremely hungry; so is the Barasana boy (who is not only kept on a restricted diet but is made to vomit up his food).

The 'bird-nester' is asphyxiated with the stench of rotten lizards; the Barasana boy is covered with black paint – paint which 'is the colour of rottenness and death, and makes the wearer dead'.[77] The 'bird-nester's' rear is devoured by vultures, so that, in the absence of a rectum, all his food passes straight through; the Barasana boy's anus is 'opened up' as he drinks the diarrhoea-inducing beer. The 'bird-nester' stops himself up with an artificial behind made of dough; the Barasana boy is taught 'control over bodily orifices' – that is, taught how to become 'stopped up' as an essential aspect of his education (which involves being alternately open' and 'closed' in accordance with definite rules).[78] The 'bird-nester's' adventures immediately precede the onset of a thunderstorm which extinguishes almost all fire; *He* House immediately precedes the onset of the annual rains. The 'bird-nester's' identity is concealed as he assumes the form of a lizard; the Barasana boy undergoes 'skin-change' and is said to be 'like' various animals as he is concealed from his younger siblings and female kin. The 'bird-nester' is brought down from the sky and 'wakes up'; the Barasana boy finally emerges from his seclusion and from his trance-like state of temporary 'death'. The 'bird-nester' restores his own powers and uses them against his parents' generation; the Barasana boy finally emerges from his ordeal as a socially- mature man who need defer no longer to the adult world. The 'bird-nester' ends up in possession of male ritual power – which includes powers of life and death over women. He kills his father. Through his temporary 'death', the Barasana boy has been reborn with power over all women – including his mother – and with the prospect of standing in his father's social place.

A seemingly plausible fit can, then, be claimed. Yet if this is so, it's not because of anything special about the 'bird-nester' story – it can be shown that countless other myths might have served in its place. Suppose the Barasana had to make do with the story of Little Red Riding Hood or Jack-and-the-Beanstalk. They would surely find a way of interpreting these, too, in terms of *He* House.

Little Red Riding Hood and He House

Let's take Little Red Riding Hood. A Barasana boy might feel that he was – in becoming initiated – taking the part of the heroine in the story. He would be playing the role of a girl. This would not necessarily seem unnatural: to the extent that they are 'menstruating' and 'giving birth', all the participants in *He* House are men playing female roles. The girl's red cap might seem significant: obviously – it might be assumed – it referred to the red paint used in the rite. The 'false grandmother' might also seem disturbingly familiar: the 'Mother' who is really a sinister male might seem uncannily reminiscent of the boy's somewhat frightening male relatives – including his father – claiming to offer intimate contact with 'menstrual blood' and Vagina Woman's womb. By the same token, Red Riding Hood's becoming swallowed alive might also seem perfectly familiar, for doesn't a boy in *He* House get swallowed by a giant snake? Finally, the episode in which the wolf's belly is slit open and its victims released might be read as an obvious reference to what happens at the end of *He* House, when everyone emerges from womb-like seclusion and returns to normal life.

Jack-and-the-Beanstalk and He House

Jack-and-the-Beanstalk might seem to the Barasana familiar in much the same way. Jack obtains magical beans from his mother or grandmother; all magic among the Barasana has similarly been obtained from an ancestral mother figure (Vagina-Woman). Jack shows incontinence in bleeding from the nose; the Barasana boy undergoing initiation is painted red, and experiences diarrhoea. Jack is hungry; so is the participant in *He* House. In the giant's house, Jack seems a miniscule figure; he is popped into the giant's oven. The young participant in *He* House is said to be reduced to the size of a foetus; he is secluded in a special small compartment within the communal house. The giant smells Jack's blood and wants to eat him; the Barasana boy is covered in symbolic menstrual blood and is swallowed by a snake. Jack escapes, stealing a trophy, and repeats this three times. For three days, a Barasana boy remains in *He* House; he gains magic trophies which were stolen from women at the beginning of time. Jack blackens his face before climbing the beanstalk; a boy in *He* House undergoes 'skin-change' associated with being painted black. Jack chops down the beanstalk; *He* House comes to an end. The world outside *He* House seems as far removed from the world inside as the earth seems from the sky.

Conclusion

The Barasana, then, have their own rich corpus of myths which clarify the logic of their rituals. It might have been rewarding to have studied them here. Yet there is no need. For our purposes it hardly seems to matter precisely which magical myths are selected as keys through which to understand rites such as *He* House. The myths are all products of the same general logic, and can be made to function more or less equally well.

In fact, the Barasana would probably feel at home not only with many of Grimm's fairy-tales, but also with the myths of Aboriginal Australia or with much of the mythology of ancient Greece. They could certainly draw significant comparisons with their own mythology – which itself is not a rigid doctrine of faith but a fluid social awareness, rich in contradictions, disputes and variations, and expressed through an indefinite number of myths and tales which have been overheard from neighbouring tribes, borrowed, exchanged, incorporated into more familiar tales, half-forgotten, distorted and amended in the manner common to story-tellers throughout the world. There is no rigid, point-by-point, inevitable correspondence between any one particular myth and any one particular ritual tradition. Rather, a basically lunar logic – that of the template central to my argument – is at a deep level governing the practice of magical ritual everywhere, the operation of this logic spinning off ritual practices and fairy tales in an endless variety of forms. If there can always be discovered an impressively precise correspondence between any one spin-off and any other – whether between myth and myth, myth and rite or one rite and another – it need not be because of any special relationship between them. No one myth need stay anchored to one ritual, nor need any one localised ritual be explained by any one myth or set of myths. All are at the deepest level equally illuminating of one another because they all lead back to the same logical source. As products of a single lunar generator of collective thought and practice, all are, from an external patriarchal standpoint, absurdity or lunacy of much the same general kind.

Notes

1 Adapted from 'Little Briar Rose', *The Complete Grimm's Fairy Tales*, 1975. Routledge, pp. 237-41.
2 Bettelheim, B. 1978. *The uses of enchantment. The meaning and importance of fairy tales.* Harmondsworth: Penguin, p. 232.
3 Lyle, E. 1986. Archaic calendar structure approached through the principle of Isomorphism. *Semiotics* 61, 3/4: 243-57; p. 243.
4 Murray, M. A. 1921. *The witch-cult in western Europe.* Oxford: University Press, p. 16.
5 Knight, C. 1987. Menstruation and the Origins of Culture. A reconsideration of Lévi-Strauss's work on symbolism and myth. Unpublished Ph.D. thesis. University of London, London. See especially Chapter 5.
6 See Frontispiece: the Lunar Template.
7 Fenwick, H. 1796. *Round about our coal fire: or Christmas entertainments.* London (reprint of 4th edition, 1734), pp. 32-45.
8 Opie and Opie 1980. *The classic fairy tales.* St. Albans: Granada, pp. 214-26.
9 Opie and Opie, p. 213.
10 Opie and Opie, p. 212.
11 Knight. See especially Chapter 5.
12 Opie and Opie, pp. 214-226.
13 See for example Read, K. E. 1966. *The High Valley.* London: Allen & Unwin, p. 131. For a psychoanalytical perspective, see Bettelheim, B. 1955. *Symbolic Wounds.* London: Thames and Hudson.
14 For Aboriginal story-tellers in North East Arnhem Land, Australia, Yurlunggur is the name of the rainbow-snake. It is aroused by the smell of blood, roars like thunder and swallows people alive. See Warner, W. L. 1957, *A Black Civilization.* New York: Harper, pp. 234-301.
15 Knight, chapters 6 and 11.
16 As above, chapter 5.
17 Zipes, J. 1983. *The trials and tribulations of Little Red Riding Hood.* London: Heinemann, pp. 28-9.
18 Knight, chapter 5.
19 Zipes, p. 28.
20 The same.
21 Zipes, p. 29.

22 Zipes, p. 30.
23 Bettelheim, p. 179.
24 Opie and Opie, p. 152.
25 Abridged from Opie and Opie, pp. 161-65
26 Cox, M. R. 1893. *Cinderella: three hundred and forty-five variants*. London: The Folk-Lore Society.
27 Cox, pp. 490-98
28 Cox p. 128
29 Cox p. 142
30 Cox p. xxxvi
31 Cox p. 144
32 Cox provides 345 versions.
33 *The Complete Grimm's Fairy-Tales*, London: Routledge, p. 126.
34 Dundes, A. 1980. *Interpreting Folklore*. Bloomington: Indiana University Press, p. 47
35 *The Complete Grimm's Fairy-Tales*, p. 127.
36 Cox pp. 490-98
37 Cox pp. 490-98.
38 Cox.
39 *Grimm and Grimm*, p. 124
40 Lévi-Strauss 1970. *The raw and the cooked (Introduction to a science of mythology 1)*. London: Cape, pp. 35-37.
41 Lévi-Strauss 1970, pp. 124-135
42 Hugh-Jones, S. 1979. *The palm and the pleiades. Initiation and cosmology in northwest Amazonia*. Cambridge: University Press, pp. 200-201.
43 Crocker, J. C. 1985. *Vital souls, Bororo cosmology, natural symbolism, and shamanism*. Tucson, Arizona: University of Arizona Press, pp. 66, 106.
44 Lévi-Strauss 1973. *From honey to ashes (Introduction to a science of mythology 2)*. London: Cape, pp. 414-15.
45 Hugh-Jones, S. p. 200.
46 Hugh-Jones, C. 1979. *From the milk river: spatial and temporal processes in northwest Amazonia*. Cambridge: University Press, pp. 200-01.
47 Hugh-Jones, S. p. 266.
48 Hugh-Jones, S. pp. 163-192.

49 Hugh-Jones, S. p. 184.
50 Hugh-Jones, S. p. 76.
51 Hugh-Jones, C., p. 153.
52 Hugh-Jones, S. p. 132.
53 Hugh-Jones, S. p. 132.
54 Hugh-Jones, S. p. 218.
55 Hugh-Jones, S. p. 184.
56 Hugh-Jones, C. p. 149.
57 Hugh-Jones, S. p. 77.
58 Hugh-Jones, S. p. 120.
59 Hugh-Jones, S. p. 183.
60 Hugh-Jones, S. p. 83.
61 Hugh-Jones, C. p. 155.
62 Hugh-Jones, S. p. 178.
63 Hugh-Jones, S. p. 263.
64 Hugh-Jones, S. p. 179.
65 Hugh-Jones, S. p. 192.
66 Reichel-Dolmatoff, G. 1968. *Amazonian cosmos. The sexual and religious symbolism of the Tukano Indians.* Chicago & London: University of Chicago Press, p. 74.
67 Hugh-Jones, C. p. 156.
68 Hugh-Jones, C. p. 156.
69 Hugh-Jones, S. p. 264.
70 Hugh-Jones, S. p. 250.
71 Hugh-Jones, S. pp. 264-5.
72 Hugh-Jones, S. p. 182.
73 Hugh-Jones, S. pp. 264-5.
74 Hugh-Jones, S. p. 274.
75 Hugh-Jones, C. p. 153.
76 Hugh-Jones, S. p. 222.
77 Hugh-Jones, C. p. 149.
78 Hugh-Jones, S. p. 202.

By the same author:

BLOOD RELATIONS:
MENSTRUATION AND THE ORIGINS OF CULTURE
1991 New Haven and London: Yale University Press

"This book may be the most important ever written on the evolution of human social organization. It brings together observation and theory from social anthropology, primatology, and paleoanthropology in a manner never before equalled."
Alex Walter, *Anthropology, Rutgers University*

"*Blood Relations* is an extraordinary work, in which imaginary creatures and magical events are orchestrated on a global scale, from Australia to Amazonia, into a single vision of how humans created humanity…."
Marek Kohn, *Independent on Sunday*

"A most important, novel, well-argued and monumental piece of work."
J. D. Lewis-Williams, *Rock Art Research Unit, University of the Witwatersrand*

"This is truly a magnificent work that will influence all human sciences for a long time to come. Scholarly, well written, a landmark that subverts the field."
Mario Rendon, *Amazon.com reviewer*

"The Most Brilliant Anthropological Study Ever Written. The many words used to describe Chris Knight's *Blood Relations* include, monumental, encyclopedic, brilliant, original, ingenious, and a tour-de-force. It is all of these and more! This work is simply the most brilliant and imaginative book about human cultural development ever written."
Anonymous, *Amazon.com reviewer*

"…a fully social and revolutionary account of our human cultural origins that privileges women; an explicitly political narrative of science in the first person; an interweaving of anthropology, biology, history of ideas, and philosophy; an attempt not just to interpret the world but to change the world: *Blood Relations* is all this and more".
Diane Bell, *American Ethnologist*

"Chris Knight has taken on the task of explicating not only the whys and hows of human cultural evolution, but also vast constellations of cultural behaviour covering Australia, Africa, Europe and all of the Americas. In this endeavour he is extraordinarily cross-disciplinary in his approach, utilizing insights from cultural anthropology, sociology, sociobiology and palaeo- and ethno-archaeology. In short, Knight is a complete anthropologist, one who realizes the value of exploring all corners of his field to synthesize disparate work into a cohesive whole… And his scholarship is impeccable. While many of us rarely bother to read 'the greats' of our field any more, Knight delves deep into Durkheim, Frazer and Lévi-Strauss and many others, coming up with long-forgotten insights and providing his readers with an enormously useful review of a century of evolutionary theory and ethnographic data… It made me review in my mind everything I ever learned about evolution and rethink it in a new way."
R. E. Davis-Floyd, *Journal of the Royal Anthropological Institute*

"Revolutions in science seldom appear ready made.... But I suspect that the basis of a new synthesis between anthropology and biology may well lie within the pages of this book."

Robin Dunbar, *Times Higher Educational Supplement*

"No, this is not another Man the Hunter origins myth, with man simultaneously inventing technology, culture and the nuclear family, and teaching it all to his dumb wife sitting at home with baby, waiting for the bacon. On the contrary. First it is not about Man or even Woman: it is about women organising in solidarity with one another. Yes, it is about culture: how women's solidarity was at the core of it. And yes, it is also about the family: how women's solidarity exploded the 'natural family' of most primate societies, in which the females are the sexual possessions of the male or males. Knight argues that the first human societies were communist. For him, as for Friedrich Engels, this means something historically specific (and nothing whatsoever to do with the monstrosity of Stalinism). Communism meant a society in which women – as never before or since – were free. Women collectively said No to rape, and men obeyed. Responsibility for children belonged to the whole community. Women's rule – matriarchy – in this sense meant freedom for everyone. Language, co-operation and science replaced physical coercion, animal individualism, and the rule of genes."

Liz Dalton, *Sulfur Magazine*

"Read this book and be changed. It is another of the great books of our time whose far-reaching influence in modern culture has not even begun to be felt."

Earl Hazell, *Amazon.com reviewer*

"One of Knight's chapters is headed 'The Revolution'..., but his whole book might well have had this in the title for his thesis has revolutionary implications for modern scholarship as well as hypothesising a revolution in the remote past."

Emily Lyle, *Scottish Studies, University of Edinburgh*

"*Blood Relations* is magnificent. Comprehensive in design, powerfully informed in execution – this book clarifies not only the problems of the past, but posits the need for a new cultural leap if we are to survive the present."

M. R. A. Chance, *Anthropology, University College London*

"Chris Knight in *Blood Relations* has this 'extraordinary resolve'. His is an immense work of documentation and close argument. For all its obvious risks, the model offers no hypothesis which is not rigorously testable. Not only this, but it appears to solve most of the outstanding conundrums in contemporary anthropology."

Peter Redgrove, *Times Literary Supplement*

"Encyclopaedic in scope, this is a seminal work that will certainly stand as a classic example of the application of the Marxist anthropological model to an examination of the origin of human culture..."

Choice, *American Library Association*

"Chris Knight has a political agenda, and he is not going to hide it from us. He is a good Marxist ('old fashioned' as some readers are bound to conclude), believing in class struggle, trade-union activism, workers' solidarity, and most of all in Engels's version of primitive communism and the early matriarchate....This theory is designed to cock a snook at every premise which sleeps undisturbed in our current assumptions....The result is an exhilaratingly original edifice of astonishing range."

Caroline Humphrey, London Review of Books

"*Blood Relations* is an incredible work of scholarship, and in particular of Marxist scholarship – a vindication of scientific socialist theory at a time when Marxism is supposed to be dead. Here we have the actual proof that Marxist theory works. Not by ignoring facts that don't fit – but by putting the facts first. The facts are sacred. The theory must fit the facts. We're so used to having paraded before us Marxism and Marxism-Leninism as it was prostituted by the Soviet Union – where if the facts didn't fit they were ignored – that we've forgotten what Marxism really means. Chris' book is based on the facts. These facts were well-known within a variety of scientific disciplines – sociology, anthropology, archaeology. You look at these facts, and a lot of them seem completely inexplicable. They appear bizarre. Why do women co-ordinate their menstrual cycles? Why do so many religions have taboos on menstruation? Why do they have taboos on eating bloody meat? And this is not just in one or two societies, but all round the world, in societies which appear to have very little else in common. Now, men were not very interested in these facts. They just seemed to be bizarre things that primitive societies did. Their importance is that they're the key to understanding how we became human.... Chris' theory may not be 100 per cent correct. But so far, it explains all the known facts. None of the other theories did. And I don't think it's too strong to say that in time to come it will be seen as significant perhaps in the way Darwin was seen as significant, in really changing the way we look at what it is to be human."

Dorothy Macedo, Campaign for Labour Party Democracy

"A quite remarkable contribution to our subject."

Marilyn Strathern, Social Anthropology, University of Manchester

"From apparently modest beginnings, this is the most ambitious project on the origins of culture to have emerged for decades. The effort to establish a collectivist point of departure for the theory of human communication has had to struggle against the individualist assumptions that dominate cognitive science, but this very struggle makes the book original and important".

Mary Douglas, C.B.E., F.B.A.

"...what I want to convey here is the excitement – and the quite extraordinary sense of homecoming and comradeship – which this magnificent book has caused me. But also relief, such relief: as if I am at last in the presence of an understanding which allows something hard and knotted and perverse and intrinsically unshareable, to unfold, stretch, breathe. The release of tension as I read page after page of the detailed, passionate and ironic argument was extraordinary, and something for which I still feel great waves of gratitude."

David Holt, Guild of Pastoral Psychologists

"How did human language and culture first emerge? The answer has now been found. It points us back to the very place where we all learned our craft. Human solidarity and culture began on the picket line."

Jim Perry, Cannock Chase & Littleton National Union of Mineworkers

ANTHROPOLOGY

AN EVENING CLASS INTRODUCTION
Chris Knight

Tuesdays 6-9 pm

Further information:
email: chris.knight@live.com
www.radicalanthropologygroup.org
www.chrisknight.co.uk